TOOTH by TOOTH

COMPARING FANGS, TUSKS, AND CHOMPERS

SARA LEVINE

ILLUSTRATIONS BY
T.S SPOOKYTOOTH

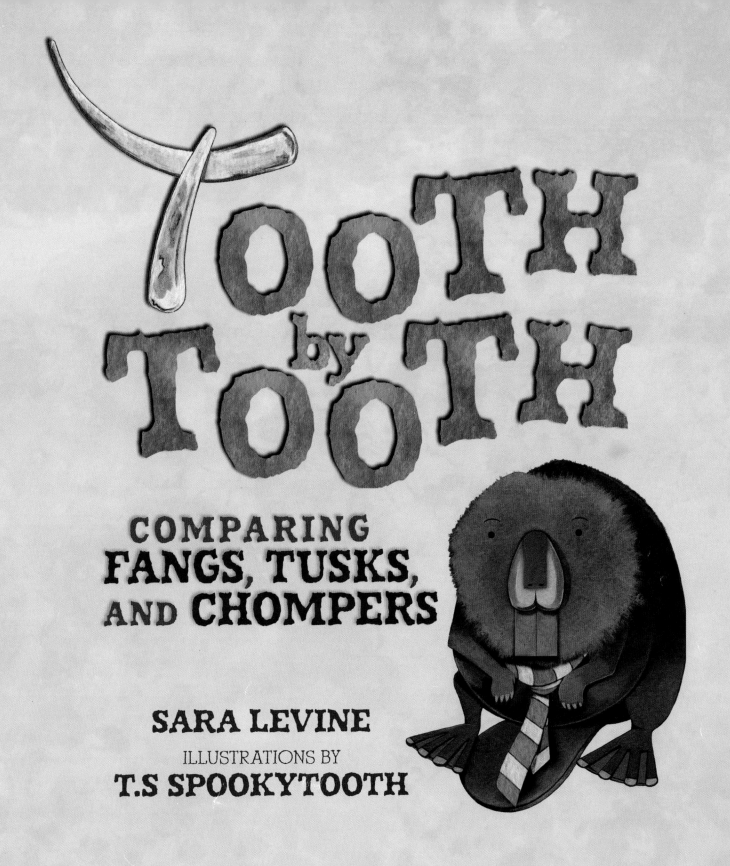

M Millbrook Press Minneapolis

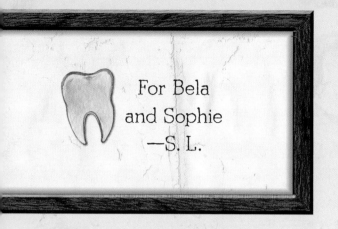

For Bela
and Sophie
—S. L.

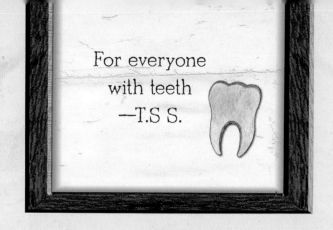

For everyone
with teeth
—T.S S.

Millbrook Press
A division of Lerner Publishing Group, Inc.
241 First Avenue North
Minneapolis, MN 55401 USA

For reading levels and more information, look up this title at www.lernerbooks.com.

Main body text set in GFY Palmer Regular 32/30 and King George Bold Clean Regular 30/31.5. Typefaces provided by Chank.

Library of Congress Cataloging-in-Publication Data

Levine, Sara (Veterinarian)
    Tooth by tooth : comparing fangs, tusks, and chompers / Sara Levine ; illustrations by T.S Spookytooth.
      pages cm.
    ISBN 978-1-4677-5215-2 (lb : alk. paper) — ISBN 978-1-4677-9727-6 (eb pdf)
     1. Teeth—Juvenile literature. 2. Anatomy, Comparative—Juvenile literature.
   3. Mammals—Juvenile literature. I. Spookytooth, T. S., illustrator. II. Title.
   QL858.L57 2016
   599.9'43—dc23
                                            2015001021

Manufactured in the United States of America
1 – CG – 12/31/15

OPEN WIDE!

Look at all those chompers in there.

Did you know your teeth are unusual? It's true! That's because you're a mammal. Lots of animals have teeth, but mammal teeth come in different shapes and sizes.

Mammals have three kinds of teeth. Take a look in a mirror and see if you can find them in your own mouth.

Do you see the flat teeth in front?

Those are your incisors. If you haven't lost any recently, you should have four on top and four on the bottom.

Structure of a tooth

crown — enamel
— dentin
— pulp
— gum
— cementum
root — blood vessels
— nerve

How many do you have?

Next to your incisors are sharp, pointy teeth. They're called canine teeth, and you have four of them in there, unless the tooth fairy visited not too long ago.

Now open up really, really wide. Way in back are your molars. You may have a lot to count in there. Depending on their age, people have anywhere from zero to twenty molars. If you are over three years old, you'll probably have at least eight.

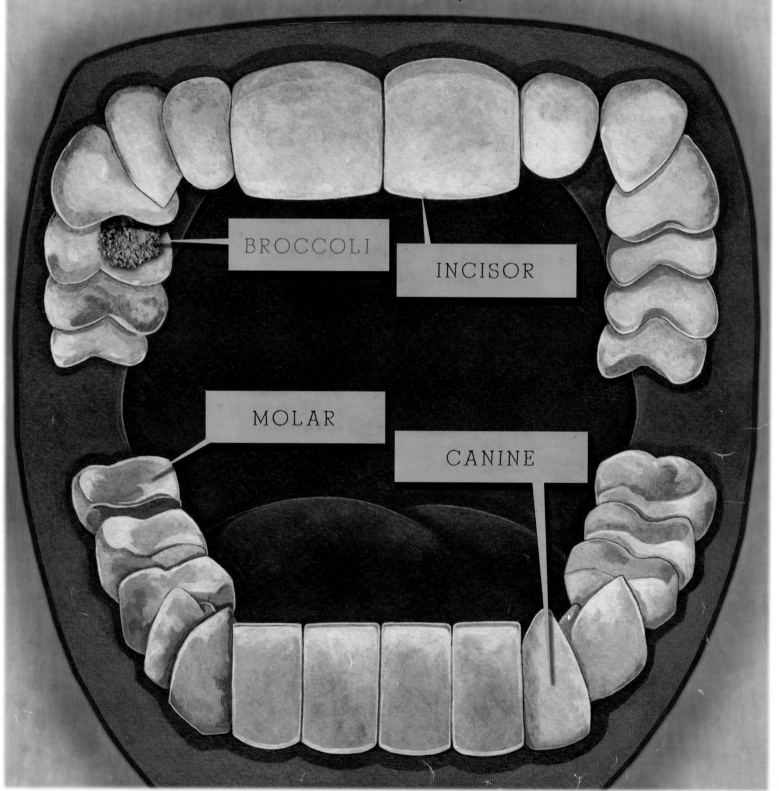

Other mammals also have incisors, canines, and molars. You can tell a lot about what a mammal eats if you look at which type of teeth are the largest in its mouth.

Imagine that your incisors were longer than your other teeth.

What kind of animal would you be if they were long enough to stick out of your mouth, even when it was closed?

A BEAVER OR A SQUIRREL OR A RABBIT!*

Mammals with really long incisors are herbivores, animals that eat only plants. These teeth are great for, say, biting into hard nuts and scraping bark from a tree.

*Some other correct answers to this question are mice, gerbils, hamsters, muskrats, woodchucks, and hares.

HAMSTER SKULL

What kind of mammal would you be if you had really long canines?

A SEAL OR A CAT OR A DOG OR A BEAR!*

Animals with big canine teeth have meat in their diet. Canine teeth are tools for killing and eating other animals. These sharp, bladelike teeth stab and tear.

DOG SKULL

Many animals with large canine teeth eat only meat, and they are called carnivores. But some of them eat plants too. Animals that eat both plants and meat are omnivores.

*Some other correct answers to this question are ferrets, raccoons, wolves, foxes, lions, and tigers.

What kind of mammal would you be if you had really tall molars?

A HORSE OR A COW OR A GIRAFFE!*

Really tall molars are good for grinding up grass and other leafy plants.

COW SKULL

These mammals are herbivores, just like the mammals with large incisors. If a mammal eats mostly plants, chances are it will have either large incisors or large molars. Since not all herbivores eat the same meals, their teeth don't all look the same.

*Some other correct answers to this question are sheep, goats, llamas, antelopes, deer, and zebras.

What kind of mammal would you be if all of your teeth—incisors, canines, and molars—were all around the same height?

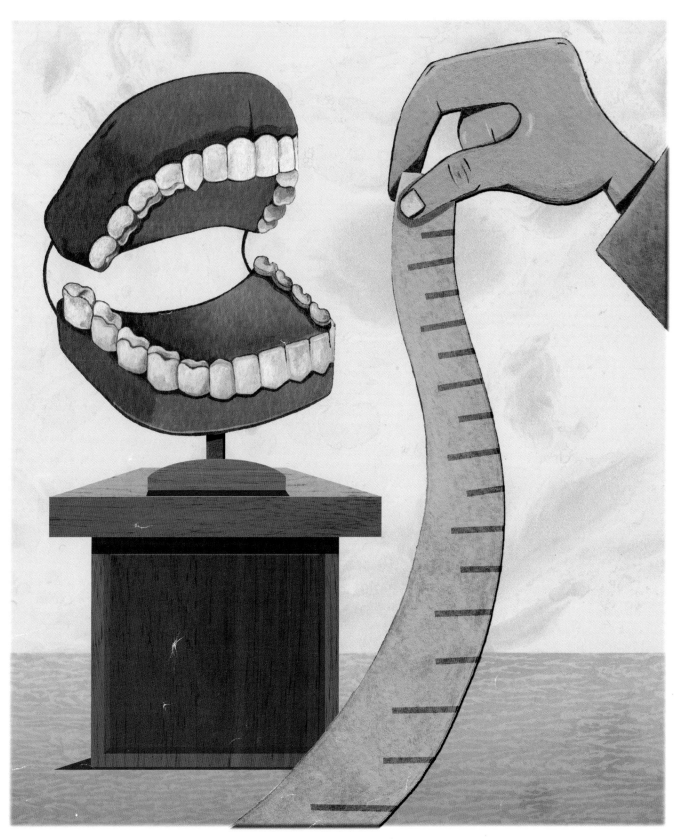

YOU'D BE YOU! A HUMAN!

Since we eat plants **and** meat for food, we need teeth that can do many different jobs. We need them because we're omnivores.

This isn't the end of the story, though. Some mammals have teeth so wacky that they aren't even used for chewing food.

AN ELEPHANT!

These enormous incisors have their own special name: tusks. Since elephants have big incisors, you can guess they probably eat plants, and you'd be right! While tusks aren't good for eating with, elephants can use them to tear bark from a tree or to dig up roots for a meal.

What kind of mammal would you be
if your top canine teeth grew almost
all the way down to your feet?

A WALRUS!

Walruses, like other animals with big canines, eat meat. While they can't use these massive teeth to chew, they do use them to poke holes in the ice to find their favorite foods: oysters and clams. After diving down for a meal, walruses can use their tusks to pull themselves back up onto the ice for a nap.

What kind of mammal would you be if your top **and** bottom canine teeth curled up out of your mouth so you had two pairs of tusks?

A WARTHOG!

A warthog's lower tusks become razor sharp from rubbing against the upper ones each time the warthog opens and closes its mouth. It's like they have a knife sharpener in their mouths. They use these fancy teeth for digging, fighting, and defending themselves against predators such as lions and leopards.

What kind of mammal would you be if you had one upper canine tooth so long that it grew through your upper lip and kept growing until it was longer than your entire body?

A MALE NARWHAL!*

The purpose of this tusk is a mystery scientists are trying to solve. Here's one thing they do know: the outside of the tusk is very sensitive. And narwhals may use it to get information about the world in much the same way that you use your eyes and your ears and your nose.

*Some female narwhals also have tusks, but theirs are smaller.

What kind of mammal would you be if you never grew any teeth at all?

AN ANTEATER OR A PANGOLIN!

These animals eat bugs—mostly ants and termites. They don't need teeth because they can slurp up their prey with their sticky tongues and swallow them whole. Small pebbles and sand in their stomachs help grind up their food. How do the pebbles and sand get in there? They slurp them up too!

What about animals that aren't mammals?
What about their teeth?

Some fish, amphibians, and reptiles have teeth. But their teeth aren't nearly as varied. They are all around the same shape. And they are all around the same height. In fact, since these teeth are so similar, they don't even have special names. No incisors. No canine teeth. No molars. Certainly no tusks.*

KOMODO
DRAGON

FROG

*Venomous snakes are an exception. They have fangs:
long, pointy teeth used for paralyzing prey.

What do you think you would look like if you had teeth like a reptile or a fish or an amphibian?

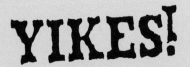

YIKES! It wouldn't be very pretty. And your lunch options would likely be very, very different.

But don't worry—that's not going to happen. Relax and enjoy your sandwich. You have mammal teeth, so you can crunch on your carrot and celery sticks too.

Done with your lunch?
Good. Smile, then, so we can take one last look at your fancy chompers.

MORE ABOUT MAMMALS

You know that mammals are different from other animals with bones because they have teeth in different shapes and sizes, but how else can you tell if a vertebrate is a mammal?

Does the mother make milk for her babies? If so, it's a mammal.

Do you see hair or fur on its body? Then it's a mammal. (Cool fact: dolphins don't look like they have hair or fur, but they are still mammals. Here's why: when baby dolphins are born, they have a "mustache" of hair that helps them to find their mothers to nurse. But this falls out when they get older!)

Are there three special bones inside its ear for hearing? If so, it's a mammal.

MORE ABOUT MAMMAL TEETH

Did you know that most mammals have two sets of teeth: milk teeth (also known as baby teeth or deciduous teeth) and adult teeth (also known as permanent teeth)? Milk teeth are the first ones that a mammal has, and they are smaller versions of the adult ones. Once the baby mammal stops nursing, milk teeth usually fall out and larger teeth grow in.

Most mammals are born with their baby teeth. But some, like humans, don't get them until after they are born. And in some mammals such as seals and rabbits, the milk teeth fall out even before they are born!

GLOSSARY

canine tooth: a pointed tooth in a mammal's mouth. These teeth are also sometimes called eyeteeth or fangs.

carnivore: an animal that eats only meat

fang: a long, pointed tooth

herbivore: an animal that eats only plants

incisor: a flat tooth in the front of a mammal's mouth

mammal: a vertebrate that has hair or fur, makes milk for its babies, has three middle ear bones, and usually has differently shaped teeth in its mouth

milk teeth: a temporary set of smaller teeth found in most mammals. They fall out, and then the adult teeth come in. Milk teeth are also known as baby teeth or deciduous teeth.

molar: a wide tooth with ridges in the back of a mammal's mouth

omnivore: an animal that eats both plants and meat

predator: an animal that hunts and eats other animals

prey: an animal hunted by another animal for food

tooth: a small, hard, whitish structure found in the mouth of many vertebrates used for chewing food and sometimes for other purposes too

tusk: a very long mammal tooth that sticks out of the mouth

vegetarian: a human who chooses to eat only plants. Since vegetarians are humans, they are also omnivores because they still have teeth that are shaped to eat both plants and meat.

vertebrate: an animal with bones. Animals that have bones include fish, amphibians, reptiles, mammals, and birds.

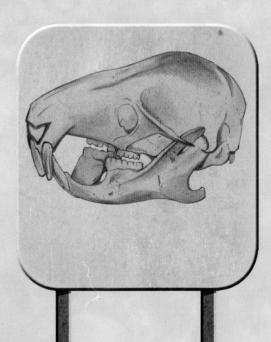

FURTHER READING

Books

Collard, Sneed B., III. *Teeth*. Watertown, MA: Charlesbridge, 2008.
  Peek inside the mouths of animals, including a great white shark and a Cuban crocodile, to see what their teeth look like.

Keller, Laurie. *Open Wide: Tooth School Inside*. New York: Henry Holt, 2000.
  Take a trip to Tooth School and learn about how to take care of your teeth from Dr. Flossman.

Markle, Sandra. *What If You Had Animal Teeth!?* New York: Scholastic, 2013.
  This book explores what sorts of superhuman feats you would be able to accomplish if you had animal teeth.

Randolph, Joanne. *Whose Teeth Are These?* New York: Rosen, 2009.
Can you match the teeth to the animal? Explore different shapes and sizes of teeth, and find out which set of teeth belongs to which animal.

Websites

CBBC Newsround—Animal Teeth
http://news.bbc.co.uk/cbbcnews/hi/find_out/guides/tech/teeth/newsid_3830000/3830561.stm
Discover fun facts about animal teeth at this site. Check out the links for information about milk teeth, tooth decay, taking care of your teeth, and more.

KidsHealth—Your Teeth
http://kidshealth.org/kid/htbw/teeth.html#
Find out about the different parts of your teeth, the different types of teeth, and how to keep your teeth healthy.

Science Kids—Teeth and Eating
http://www.sciencekids.co.nz/gamesactivities/teetheating.html
This website features interactive games that will help you learn more about why different animals have different types of teeth and how these teeth are suited for their diets.